ENDOI

M000012291

"You probably know that, if you are a Christian, the Holy Spirit came into your life to live out the life of Jesus Christ. Without the indwelling presence of God's Holy Spirit, the Christian life is impossible. Kurt has helped us as Christians to understand the Spirit's presence in us, and His power through us, as we walk in fellowship with our Lord and Savior. This is a great book about the presence and power of God through each of us on a daily basis. It will help us as we learn to walk and serve Jesus Christ daily. A must-read as you walk with your Savior and Lord."

John Maisel, Author, Founder and
Chairman Emeritus of East-West

"I've never read a more succinct, encouraging, instructive book about the Holy Spirit! After studying the biblical references to the Holy Spirit—and after years of meditating on them—Kurt Nelson has packed them into a set of invigorating pages I'm going to read and reread. There's something about the biblical truths of the Holy Spirit that relaxes my heart and energizes my strength. You'll find divine secrets here—in 'Awakening to the Holy Spirit.'"

Robert J. Morgan, Author of "The Red Sea Rules,"
"The Jordan River Rules," and "God Works
All Things Together for Your Good"

"I have felt much of my adult Christian life that there has not been enough teaching on the Holy Spirit. As a child and through boarding school, the Holy Spirit was referred to as the Holy Ghost, so I wasn't exactly drawn to Him. Ghosts weren't good, so why would I seek this kind of presence for my life? Then as I matured in faith and learned more about Him, I began to realize He, too, was a Person. That this Person of the Godhead was important and was given to all who believe in Jesus Christ.

"This is exactly what Kurt Nelson, President and CEO of East-West, has written about in his book 'Awakening to the Holy Spirit.' With great insight and simplicity, Kurt helps you understand who the Holy Spirit is and how to live your Christian life with the daily awareness of His presence and power. By the end of this book the mystery is gone, and you become aware of the purpose of the Holy Spirit. Thank you, Kurt, for bringing a sensible understanding of His role in our lives as we follow the path of Jesus awaiting His return. I pray this book will bless others as it has blessed me."

Gigi Graham, Author, eldest daughter of Billy and Ruth Graham

"We have seen our friend, Kurt Nelson, abide with and lean on the Holy Spirit through the darkest of times. Our Father in Heaven has given His Spirit to dwell in us, the comforting presence that sustains and provides the power of God in the weak frames of men. This book is rich in helping us to have a greater understanding of this treasure in earthen vessels. The Holy Spirit is the miracle that has blessed us here on Earth with everything we need in the heavenly realms."

Shane & Shane, Worship Artists,
The Worship Initiative

"I've always referred to the Holy Spirit as our 'Day-to-Day Operational Manager.' Yet, I've struggled to bring Him into my daily life. After reading Kurt Nelson's book, now I know how. The title says it all! Read this book and you will awaken to the Holy Spirit in your life.

Ken Blanchard, Co-Author of "The One Minute
Manager" and "Lead Like Jesus"

"In 'Awakening to the Holy Spirit,' Kurt Nelson welcomes his readers into a character study of the Holy Spirit as portrayed throughout the Bible. Leaning on rich scriptural references throughout the Old and New Testaments, Nelson reminds us of the Holy Spirit's role and resources available to all believers by exhorting his readers to daily step into intentional relationship with the Person of the Holy Spirit as our Helper and the One who shapes us further into Christlikeness."

Mark Yarbrough, President of Dallas Theological Seminary

"I highly recommend Kurt Nelson's practical, brief, and Scripture-packed explanation of the work of the Holy Spirit in 'Awakening to the Holy Spirit.' In our academic and very cognitive-focused Christianity here in the United States, it seems that many people end up following a set of principles, and trying very hard to be a good person, as opposed to relating to the actual Person of the Holy Spirit, drawing on His power, and seeing the supernatural results that take place in and through us. I love the personal note at the end, which provides a practical way to experience the power, presence, and Person of God, the Holy Spirit, dwelling within us."

Chip Ingram, Teacher, Pastor, and Author
of "Living On the Edge"

"Many have never studied and are afraid to ask about the Holy Spirit, despite the Bible's extensive coverage of the Holy Spirit. Kurt Nelson's excellent devotional collects all the Scriptures on the subject and pulls them together, so every true believer can live a life more full of the Spirit."

Kelly Shackelford, President and CEO of First Liberty Institute

"This book is not about theology, but about a Person—the 'forgotten Person' of the Godhead, the Holy Spirit. Kurt Nelson speaks about the Spirit, not only from the truth of God's Word but with the firsthand veracity that can only come out of a personal relationship and lived experience with the Spirit of the Living God. In short, this book serves as a much-needed introduction to our Friend, the Comforter, whom Jesus promised to send us—and therefore the One whom we all so desperately need to come to know."

Bill Hendricks, Executive Director for Christian
Leadership at The Hendricks Center at Dallas Theological
Seminary, President of the Giftedness Center

"Kurt Nelson has written a wonderfully insightful book on the Holy Spirit! I am so grateful for his life and his testimony for Christ."

June Hunt, Founder and Chief Servant
Officer of Hope for the Heart

"Kurt Nelson has written a small book that will have life-changing impact. In 'Awakening the Holy Spirit,' you will read about the Person, power, presence, and purpose of the Holy Spirit. Whether this is new information or an affirmation of what you know about the One whom Jesus sent, it will encourage and embolden you. This book will also inform and remind you of what Jesus said about the Holy Spirit–the One who will make everything plain and remind you of all the things He taught us. I can hardly wait for you to read more about Him. Read this book and come alongside the One who comes alongside you."

Phyllis Hendry Halverson, President Emeritus, Lead Like
Jesus and Co-Author, "Lead Like Jesus Revisited"

"My friend Kurt Nelson is a visionary and a lifelong learner. Upon realizing just how frequently the Bible mentions the Holy Spirit, he compiled this booklet that walks through what the Bible says about the Holy Spirit, step-by-step. This is a wonderful introduction for Christians wanting a scriptural guide to know the Holy Spirit better."

Eric Metaxas, New York Times Best Selling Author and Host of the nationally syndicated Eric Metaxas Radio Show

"The Holy Spirit is always present with believers in our very being, yet we are not constantly aware of this truth. 'Awakening to the Holy Spirit' provides a short but comprehensive teaching of what the whole Bible says about the Holy Spirit, but the chapters are short, topical, easy-to-read. This is a book that should be carried with us. As we have short times of waiting in our day, it is perfect for reading a chapter in five minutes or less to remind us of the truth that is always with us but not always recognized."

Brad Smith, President, Bakke Graduate University

AWAKENING
to the HOLY
SPIRIT

His Person, Presence, Power,
and Purpose in our Lives

DR. KURT NELSON
Foreword by Randy Alcorn

Awakening to the Holy Spirit:
His Person, Presence, Power, and Purpose in Our Lives
Kurt Nelson

Published by East-West
Copyright © 2018, 2021, 2022, 2023 by East-West Publishing

Cover Photography by Toa Heftiba
unsplash.com

Printed in the United States of America

ISBN (Print): 978-1-7374997-3-2
ISBN (Ebook): 978-1-7374997-4-9

CONTENTS

FOREWORD

My friend, Kurt Nelson, has written a succinct, penetrating, and powerful treatment on the Holy Spirit. It is remarkable in that it's so drenched in Scripture that I can say a very large part of it is inspired and without error! Kurt's part isn't inerrant, but the close attention he pays to basing his words on God's Words makes this not just one more opinion piece but a concise and authoritative treatment of the Person and work of the Holy Spirit, the most neglected member of the triune God. Most of us know far less about the Holy Spirit than the Father and the Son, but we need to see Him and His work with new wonder and appreciation. I highly recommend this book!

Randy Alcorn, Author and Founder of
Eternal Perspectives Ministries

INTRODUCTION

I believe that all spiritual awakening—in our personal lives and around the world—starts with the Holy Spirit.

A few years ago, I had the privilege of reading through the Bible in 90 days, and, as I did, I was astonished at the frequency of the mentioning of the Holy Spirit. Did you know that the Holy Spirit is mentioned 90 times in the Old Testament? I had no idea! The Holy Spirit is also mentioned more than 230 times in the New Testament. That's more than 320 references to the Holy Spirit in the Word of God.

In this book, I'd like to share more about what I have discovered as I have studied what the Bible has to say about God the Holy Spirit. My hope is that it encourages you as you experience Him shaping you further into Christlikeness and fueling you to fulfill the mission He has for your life—in the power of the Holy Spirit!

GETTING TO KNOW THE HOLY SPIRIT

If you're a Christian, I'm sure you are crystal clear on the reality that we serve one true God who exists as three Persons in the mystery of the Godhead. The Westminster Confession of Faith, which was written in 1646 as a confession of basic Christian belief, states this about the mystery of the Godhead:

> "In the unity of the Godhead, there be three Persons of one substance, power, and eternity; God the Father, God the Son, and God the Holy Spirit."

If you were to be quizzed on your knowledge of God as Father, God as Son, and God as Holy Spirit, how would you do on your knowledge of the Person and the work of the Holy Spirit? How well would you say that you know

God the Father? How well would you say you know God as the Son, Jesus?

Well, I'm embarrassed to say that even as a seminary graduate and having followed Jesus for more than 50 years, I would score miserably on my knowledge of the Person and work of God the Holy Spirit. Well, at least until I began reading through the Scriptures with fresh eyes and a fresh desire to better know God as the Holy Spirit.

My observation of the Holy Spirit's prevalence in Scripture as I read through the Bible in 90 days provoked me to take a deeper look. Sadly, I've allowed myself to be influenced by church culture, theological debate, doctrinal extremes, and abuses.

In doing so, I've failed to seek to know and understand the Person and work of the Holy Spirit as I should. Frankly, I need to continue growing my knowledge of God as Father, of Jesus the Son, and of the Holy Spirit. The great news is that God's Word says we can make strides in getting to know God better. We can grow in our knowledge of God.

> *"You will seek Me and find Me when you search for Me with all your heart. I will be found by you,' declares the Lord ... ."* -Jeremiah 29:13-14, NASB

God wants you to discover Him, and if you make the effort, He says, "I'm findable. I'm discoverable." Read and meditate on this prayer from the Apostle Paul:

> *"'We continually ask God to fill you with the knowledge of his will through all the wisdom and understanding that the Spirit gives, so that you may live a life worthy of the Lord and please him in every way: bearing fruit in every good work, growing in the knowledge of God … .'" -Colossians 1:9-10*

I think these two things—bearing fruit and growing in the knowledge of God—go hand in hand. You're not going to see the life that Paul prays for without the growth and the knowledge of God that he also prays for. I hope these next few pages serve merely as an appetizer to knowing God the Holy Spirit that will cause all of us to hunger and thirst to know Him—His Person and His works—better in the days ahead.

MIRACLES OF THE HOLY SPIRIT

As I wrote these words, I wanted to share a story of the Holy Spirit at work in a humble human life. Three true stories came to mind.

I could tell you of an elderly Russian woman in Riga Latvia who was miraculously and instantly healed of emphysema and grotesquely swollen arms and legs after she prayed to receive Jesus Christ as her Savior. Or I could tell you about 12-year-old Sveta in Zaporizhia in southern Ukraine who, immediately upon trusting Jesus Christ, was healed of a horrible stutter that she had had for a year, all because her mother forced her to kiss her father's corpse in the casket at his funeral. Or I could tell you of the Hindu man in Andhra Pradesh whose leg was suddenly paralyzed as he was kicking his Hindu wife for putting her faith in Jesus Christ. And then days later he was miraculously healed when he, too, put his faith in Jesus Christ.

What's interesting about these actual stories from the mission field is that, in each case, miraculous healing followed and confirmed the greater miracle of salvation through faith in Jesus Christ.

After the miracles of the incarnation, the resurrection, and the Day of Pentecost, I believe that the greatest miracle known to man occurs each and every day when the Holy Spirit invades a dark, imprisoned human heart. They are set free through the gospel of grace and are transferred from the Kingdom of Darkness to the Kingdom of Light—the Kingdom of God's beloved Son (Colossians 1:13).

This miracle is occurring tens of thousands of times every day. I've experienced that miracle firsthand, and, if you know Jesus Christ as your Savior, so have you. As we know, that miracle changes everything.

I think the second greatest miracle that occurs in each of our lives every day is when the Holy Spirit humbles Himself to daily indwell weak and broken vessels like you and me. He overflows us with His presence, His power, His fruitfulness, and His supernatural gifts and fruits in order that we would serve Him and love Him well.

THE PURPOSE AND PRIORITY OF THE HOLY SPIRIT

Here's my thesis regarding the Holy Spirit: In order to awaken ourselves to the heart and work of God—to know Him and make Him known—we must first awaken ourselves to the Person, the presence, the power, and the purpose of the Holy Spirit in our lives.

To get us started, I want to show you His purpose in the mystery of the Godhead based on the Scriptures.

1. The purpose of the Holy Spirit's ministry in the Godhead is to glorify God the Father and to glorify Jesus Christ (John 16:14-15).

2. The Holy Spirit empowers and purifies followers of Jesus, therefore building up the Church—His Bride (Acts 4:31; Romans 15:16).

3. Through our witness, the Word of God, and the power of the Holy Spirit, unbelievers are convicted and converted to become disciples of Jesus Christ (Acts 2:38-39, 16:14).

These three points are the purpose and priority of the Holy Spirit in the Godhead. As you can see, our relationship with the Holy Spirit is absolutely essential to our ability to follow Jesus and live a Christ-like, God-honoring life.

Please note that we are expected to obey these commands given to us by Jesus Christ relating to the Holy Spirit.

> *"'Therefore go and make disciples of all nations, baptizing them in the name of the Father and of the Son and of the Holy Spirit ... .'" -Matthew 28:19*

This well-known commission challenges us, exhorts us, and commands us to baptize new believers in the name of the Father and of the Son and of the Holy Spirit.

> *"On one occasion, while he was eating with them, he gave them this command: 'Do not leave Jerusalem, but wait for the gift my Father promised, which you have heard me speak about.'" -Acts 1:4*

In this command, Jesus told the early disciples to wait until they're clothed with the Holy Spirit from on high.

> *"And with that he breathed on them and said, 'Receive the Holy Spirit.'" -John 20:22*

> *"So I say, walk by the Spirit, and you will not gratify the desires of the flesh." -Galatians 5:16*

> *"Since we live by the Spirit, let us keep in step with the Spirit." -Galatians 5:25*

> *"And do not grieve the Holy Spirit of God, with whom you were sealed for the day of redemption." -Ephesians 4:30*

> *"Do not get drunk on wine, which leads to debauchery. Instead, be filled with the Spirit ... ." -Ephesians 5:18*

> *"Do not quench the Spirit." -1 Thessalonians 5:19*

As you can see, we're commanded to receive the Holy Spirit, to walk by the Spirit, to keep in step with the Spirit, to not grieve the Holy Spirit, to be continually filled and controlled by the Holy Spirit, and to not quench or put out the Holy Spirit's fire in our lives.

With the weight of these commands in mind, let us begin to awaken ourselves afresh to the Person, the presence, the power, and the purpose of the Holy Spirit in our lives and in our individual and corporate service to the Lord.

HOW TO AWAKEN
TO THE HOLY SPIRIT

There are four things that I am convinced we must do to awaken to the Holy Spirit, including:

1. Awakening to the Person of the Holy Spirit;
2. Awakening to the presence of the Holy Spirit;
3. Awakening to the power of the Holy Spirit;
4. And awakening to the purpose of the Holy Spirit.

AWAKENING TO
THE PERSON OF
THE HOLY SPIRIT

"It is the highest importance from the standpoint
of experience that we know the Holy Spirit as a person."
-R.A. Torrey

To awaken to the Person of the Holy Spirit, a daily relationship is required.

A few years ago, I was meditating on the ministry of the
Holy Spirit in my life, and I was convicted of my own wrong
and insufficient thinking about the Holy Spirit. The Holy
Spirit is not an impersonal force, although He's forceful.
The Holy Spirit is not a mystical being, although He's full
of mystery. The Holy Spirit is not an inanimate power, although He's all-powerful. The Holy Spirit is a Person.

He's a personal being.

Just like the Father and the Son are persons, the Holy Spirit is a Person like you and me.

He has intellect. He has emotion. He has will. And the Holy Spirit is to be pursued and known and loved and related to as a Person on a daily basis, as are the Father and the Son. Here's a list of what the Scriptures say about the personal nature of the Holy Spirit.

- He walks with us (Galatians 5:25).
- He speaks to us (1 Corinthians 2:10, 14; 1 Timothy 4:1).
- He lives in us forever (John 14:16-17).
- He comforts us (John 14:16, KJV).
- He counsels us (John 14:26, AMP).
- He teaches us (John 14:26).
- He reminds us (John 14:26).
- He leads us (Galatians 5:18).
- He helps us to pray (Romans 8:26).
- He reveals truth to us (1 Corinthians 2:10).
- He cleanses us (Titus 3:5, AMP).
- He can be grieved (Ephesians 4:30).
- He gives us life (2 Corinthians 3:6).
- He carries a sword (Ephesians 6:17).
- He gives many great gifts (Romans 12, 1 Corinthians 12, Ephesians 4, 1 Peter 4).
- He fills us with God's love (Romans 5:5).

Do you see how personal these are? These wonderful gifts all come to us through the Person of God the Holy Spirit.

Seek Him, pursue Him, and get to know Him better every single day. Deepen your understanding of His Person, His workings, and His ways. The Holy Spirit is a Person.

AWAKENING TO THE PRESENCE OF THE HOLY SPIRIT

> "O Holy Spirit, descend plentifully into my heart.
> Enlighten the dark corners of this neglected
> dwelling and scatter there Thy cheerful beams."
> -Saint Augustine

Here's a rhetorical question: if you had a chance to spend an hour a day face-to-face with Jesus Christ, or an hour a day completely filled and empowered and controlled by the Holy Spirit, which would you choose? Well, Jesus actually answers this question for us when He makes this rather shocking statement.

> *"But I tell you the truth, it is better for you*
> *that I go away, for if I may not go away, the*
> *Comforter will not come unto you, and if I*

*go on, I will send Him unto you ... ." -John
16:7, YLT*

The Apostle John follows with a wonderful promise about
the Holy Spirit when he recorded, *"And [the Lord] will give
you another advocate to help you and be with you forever (John
14:16b, clarification added)."'*

Consider the entire 33 years that Jesus served the Father on
Earth. Did Jesus ever live inside Peter, James, or John? Did
Jesus ever indwell Bartholomew or any of the other Twelve,
or anybody else for that matter? The answer is an obvious,
"No." Jesus never lived inside of anybody while He lived on
this Earth.

But in John 16:7, Jesus says that, after He departs, He will
send the Holy Spirit to indwell His followers, including you
and me—nonstop, forever. Jesus said it is better for us to be
filled with the Holy Spirit than it was for His disciples to
be with Him in person. The Holy Spirit, according to these
verses, indwelt you the moment you first believed in Jesus (2
Corinthians 1:21-22, Ephesians 1:13-14, Romans 8:9). He
has never left you, and He will never leave you (John 14:16).
What an incredible promise! Jesus said it is better that He
ascend to the Father and send His Holy Spirit to live in us
and to be with us forever.

AWAKENING TO THE POWER OF THE HOLY SPIRIT

We must awaken to the Person of the Holy Spirit; we must awaken to the presence of the Holy Spirit; and third, we must awaken to the power of the Holy Spirit. "Spiritual batteries" are required and need to be recharged daily. In other words, we're spiritually dead without the Holy Spirit.

God's Word states that we have the power of the Holy Spirit available to us each and every day. It says:

- The Holy Spirit strengthens us with internal power (Ephesians 3:16).
- The Holy Spirit is described as fire (Matthew 3:11).
- The Holy Spirit is described as a violent, rushing wind (Acts 2:2).
- The Holy Spirit clothes us with power (Luke 24:49).

- The Holy Spirit grants us direct access to God the Father (Ephesians 2:18).

I don't know about you, but I want that kind of power in my life! And it gets even better. Jesus gave His followers another incredible promise that we would all experience after He sent the Holy Spirit.

> *"Very truly I tell you, whoever believes in me will do the works I have been doing, and they will do even greater things than these, because I am going to the Father." -John 14:12*

This verse is unbelievable! I wouldn't believe it except that Jesus said it, and it's in the Bible.

Jesus said that by the indwelling presence of the Holy Spirit in your life and in my life, He will do greater works in and through us than He did Himself while He was on Earth! So how does this work? How does God impart that kind of supernatural power in and through our weak, frail, and very human lives?

> "Trying to do the Lord's work in your own strength is the most confusing, exhausting, and tedious of all work. But when you are filled with the Holy Spirit, then the ministry of Jesus just flows out of you."
> -Corrie Ten Boom

I believe this transformation by the power of God only comes through humility, confession, brokenness, submission, and surrender to God on a daily basis. As we surrender ourselves to Him and, as Jesus said, we deny ourselves and take up our cross every day, God humbles Himself to overflow us with His presence and power through His indwelling Holy Spirit (Luke 9:23, Romans 8:9).

▪ THE FRUITS AND GIFTS OF THE HOLY SPIRIT

"The way I define love is by using the fruit of the Spirit, which starts with love. I believe that joy is love rejoicing, peace is love at rest, patience is love waiting, kindness is love interacting, goodness is love initiating, faithfulness is love keeping its word, gentleness is love empathizing, and self-control is love resisting temptation."
-Michael Timmis

One of the ways God fills us with His presence and power through the Holy Spirit is by giving us the fruit of the Spirit—"*love, joy, peace, patience, kindness, goodness, faithfulness, gentleness, and self-control (Galatians 5:22-23)*." These are not *your* love, *your* joy, *your* peace, *your* patience, *your* kindness, *your* goodness, *your* faithfulness, *your* gentleness, or *your* self-control that are merely improved upon by God.

These are *His* fruit, the fruit of *His* Holy Spirit manifest in and through our lives! We get to trade up for the fruit of the Spirit.

> "The way I define love is by using the fruit of the Spirit, which starts with love. I believe that joy is love rejoicing, peace is love at rest, patience is love waiting, kindness is love interacting, goodness is love initiating, faithfulness is love keeping its word, gentleness is love empathizing, and self-control is love resisting temptation." -Michael Timmis

This divine fruit is what the Holy Spirit wants to bear in and through your life as you abide in Him and allow Him to abide in you. They're all the supernatural overflow of the Holy Spirit indwelling your life.

The Holy Spirit also empowers us with supernatural gifts. The gifts listed below can be found in Romans 12:6-8, Ephesians 4:11-13, and 1 Corinthians 12:1-31.

- Administration
- Apostleship
- Discerning Spirits
- Encouraging/Exhortation
- Evangelism
- Faith

- Giving
- Healing
- Help/Service
- Interpretation
- Knowledge
- Leadership
- Mercy
- Miracles
- Pastoring
- Prophecy
- Teaching
- Tongues
- Wisdom

I want to remind us again that these are not human talents or human abilities, just like the fruits are not human either. They're supernatural. These are Holy Spirit given, supernatural empowerment for serving God and doing His ministry.

In 1 Corinthians 12:7, the Apostle Paul reminds the Corinthian believers of a critically important principle about spiritual gifts: *"Now to each one [of you] the manifestation [gifts] of the Spirit is given for the common good (clarification added)."*

"The fruit of the Spirit is fundamentally relational. Rather than originating with us, it flows to us from our union with Christ, and it flows beyond us to bring us

> into fellowship with others. The secret of this flow—
> and our unity with God and others—is humility."
> -Jerry Bridges

Here, Paul points out that spiritual gifts are not given to us for our benefit but rather for the benefit of others in the Church so that others may be built up and blessed (1 Corinthians 14:12, Ephesians 4:12). As my friend, Carol Davis, so poignantly explains, "The gifts were placed in you, but they were never meant for you!" They are meant for the edification and encouragement of your fellow believers.

Do you know what your gifts are? Are you using them to advance the Kingdom of God?

I believe that each of us has at least one of these gifts, and my experience has been that most of us have two or three spiritual gifts that the Holy Spirit manifests in and through our lives so that we may serve His Body, the lost, and the expansion of His Kingdom. But that's not all. Something else I discovered in addition to the fruit and gifts of the Spirit is that there are other vital ministries of the Holy Spirit that manifest His power in and through our lives.

The Holy Spirit also:

- Reveals the indwelling of the Father in your life (1 John 3:24).

- Reveals the indwelling of Jesus in your life (John 14:17-20, Colossians 3:11).
- Seals or guarantees our redemption (Ephesians 1:13-14).

The Holy Spirit is a Person who is present in us with immeasurable power. Christ in us through the Holy Spirit is the hope of glory (Colossians 1:27).

▪ JESUS CHRIST AND THE HOLY SPIRIT

I want to offer one final observation from the Scriptures about our need to awaken ourselves to the power of the Holy Spirit in our lives.

Jesus Christ Himself fully relied upon the presence and power of the Holy Spirit to live His own supernatural life on Earth. Jesus relied on the Holy Spirit.

Let's look at a few examples of how the Holy Spirit worked in the life of Christ:

- Conceived Jesus in the womb (Matthew 1:20, Luke 1:35)
- Anointed Jesus as Messiah at His baptism (Luke 3:22; Acts 4:27, 10:38; Hebrews 1:9)
- Filled Jesus at the start of His public ministry (Luke 4:14-21, Isaiah 61)

- Sealed Jesus as the Son of God (John 6:27)
- Led Jesus into the wilderness to be tempted by Satan (Luke 4:1)
- Always led Jesus to do the will of the Father (John 8:29)
- Gave Jesus joy (Luke 10:21)
- Empowered Jesus for ministry (Matthew 12:28; Luke 4:14-15, 18)
- Quickened Jesus at His death (1 Corinthians 15:45, KJV)

> *"'... God anointed Jesus of Nazareth with the Holy Spirit and power, and how he went around doing good and healing all who were under the power of the devil, because God was with him.'"*
> *-Acts 10:38*

Obviously the first two on this list do not apply to us, but the rest do because Jesus was filled by the Spirit at birth, and you were filled by the Spirit when you were born again.

Now here's the point of the vital relationship between Jesus Christ and the Holy Spirit: If Jesus relied on the power of the Holy Spirit to live His supernatural life on Earth, how could we dare think that we can live God-honoring and fruitful lives apart from that power working in and through our lives as we serve the Father?

The Holy Spirit is a Person with whom you must have an intimate daily relationship. He is present in you and me always, and He will never leave us. The Holy Spirit has the power that we need to live a supernatural, people-loving, lost-saving, and God-pleasing life. And, finally, the Holy Spirit has a supernatural purpose for indwelling your life and mine with His holy presence.

AWAKENING TO
THE PURPOSE OF
THE HOLY SPIRIT

Lastly, we must awaken to the purpose of the Holy Spirit in our lives. Continuous abiding in Jesus and being filled with, yielded to, and controlled by the Holy Spirit is required to fully discover that purpose!

It is essential that we understand the Holy Spirit's purposes in and through our lives if we are to cooperate with and obey Him in order to see all of God's purposes fulfilled in our lives on a daily basis.

As we saw earlier, the Holy Spirit has specific purposes or ministries in the Godhead, in the Body of Christ, and in the lives of unbelievers who hear the gospel.

- In the unity of the Godhead, the Holy Spirit serves principally to glorify God the Father and God the Son, Jesus Christ (John 16:14-15).

- In the diversity and unity of the Body of Christ, the Holy Spirit serves to indwell, empower, and gift individual believers in order to build up the Church—His Bride (Acts 4:31, Romans 15:16).
- And finally, the Holy Spirit's ministry among the lost is to convict and convert them to become disciples of Jesus Christ through God's Word and the faithful witness of Jesus' followers (Acts 2:38-39, 16:14).

In addition to these broad universal purposes of the Holy Spirit, there are several other specific purposes or ministries that the Holy Spirit fulfills in and through the lives of His people:

1. Assurance: To grant believers assurance of their new life in Christ (Romans 8:15-16; 1 John 3:24, 4:13)

2. Sanctification: To make us grow daily in our likeness to Jesus (Romans 8:13, 15:16; Galatians 5:22-23; 1 Peter 1:2; 2 Thessalonians 2:13)

3. Intercession: To pray on behalf of the spiritual welfare of God's people (Romans 8:26-27)

4. Teaching: To instruct believers in God's Word and in His ways (John 14:26, 16:13; Luke 12:12)

5. Guidance: To direct us when we need specific direction and wisdom in life and ministry (Acts 15:28, 16:6-7; Romans 8:4, 14; Galatians 5:16-18)

6. Unity: To create and maintain the unity of God's people, the Church (Ephesians 4:3, Philippians 2:1-2, 1 Corinthians 12:13)

7. Empowerment: To manifest God's supernatural life in and through His people as they serve Him (1 Corinthians 12:7-11, Ephesians 6:17)

8. Witness: To empower and make effective our bold witness for the gospel (Acts 1:8)

9. Salvation: Through the hearing of the gospel, to regenerate the spiritually dead to make them alive in Christ (John 3:5-8)

The first six purposes, or ministries, of the Holy Spirit in the lives of God's people are more inward or edifying. They build up the individual believer or the Church. The latter three–empowerment, witness, and salvation–are more outward or "reaching the unreached" focused. I believe that the first six purposes of the Holy Spirit in our lives are essentially designed to prepare us for the ministry of the gospel. They allow us to be empowered witnesses, leading to the salvation of the lost as embodied in the last three purposes of the Holy Spirit!

> "The baptism of the Spirit is God's ultimate purpose for His people. He didn't save us so we could go to Heaven. He saved us so He could fill us so full of Himself we could have intimacy with Him, we could become more like Him, and we could change the world with Him."
> -Rob Reimer

East-West's Founder, John Maisel, often reminds our team that "Jesus' mission statement was, 'I have come to seek and to save that which is lost'" (Luke 19:10). I believe that John is spot on in that observation! And if that was Jesus' primary and focal mission, for which He obediently came to Earth, then can it be any less than the mission of all Christ's followers? In fact, that same mission was reiterated by Jesus in Acts 1:8 when, inspired by the Holy Spirit, Dr. Luke recorded the final words of Jesus:

> *"But you will receive power when the Holy Spirit comes on you; and you will be my witnesses in Jerusalem, and in all Judea and Samaria, and to the ends of the earth."*

Bearing witness to Jesus and to His gospel in your hometown (your Jerusalem) and all the way to the ends of the Earth is a direct result of being filled, indwelt, and empowered by the Holy Spirit. This is the exact same mission that Jesus charged His followers with just seconds before He ascended into Heaven to sit at the right hand of God the Father for all eternity. These words were essentially Jesus' last will and testament to all who will follow Him.

I trust that you are keeping in step with the Holy Spirit as He works in your life to grant you assurance, sanctification, intercession, teaching, guidance, and unity in His Body (Galatians 5:25).

Are you also keeping in step with the Holy Spirit as He indwells and empowers you to be a faithful witness to Him and to His gospel, resulting in the spiritually lost coming to experience new life in Christ?

Jesus' mandate for us to be faithful witnesses for Him is a key purpose of the Holy Spirit living in your life and in mine. As Paul exhorted young Timothy, *"But you, be sober in all things, endure hardship, do the work of an evangelist, fulfill your ministry (2 Timothy 4:5)."*

EXPERIENCING THE HOLY SPIRIT IN YOUR LIFE

The question many may be asking at this point is, "How can I be sure that I have the Holy Spirit in my life?" That is both a great and very natural question to ask after awakening to the reality of the Holy Spirit and all of the riches of His Person, presence, power, ministries, gifts, and fruits that He offers to bring along with Himself into our lives!

▪ RECEIVING JESUS

The Bible makes it extremely clear that there is only one pathway for the Holy Spirit to enter a person's life, and that is by first placing your faith in Jesus Christ to forgive your sins and to be your Savior as a completely free gift of the love and grace of God. The promise of eternal life through faith in Jesus Christ is nowhere more famously captured than in

John 3:16: *"For God so [greatly] loved and dearly prized the world, that He [even] gave His [One and] only begotten Son, so that whoever believes and trusts in Him [as Savior] shall not perish, but have eternal life (AMP)."*

The need for salvation through faith in Jesus Christ is based upon the clear teaching of the Bible—that every man, woman, and child alive today needs forgiveness of sin from God and the free gift of eternal life:

- All of us have sinned against God our Creator, who alone is holy (Romans 3:23).
- Our sin separates us from the possibility of a relationship with a holy God and must be punished with death (Romans 6:23).
- God proves and demonstrates His love for us by sacrificing His only Son Jesus Christ in our place to pay in full for our sins (Romans 5:8, John 3:16).
- We can be fully forgiven of all our sins as a free gift from God when we place our faith in Jesus alone as our Savior (Ephesians 2:8-9, Romans 10:9-10).

It is not a prayer that saves us; it is faith in Jesus' sinless life and sacrificial death, burial, and resurrection for us that achieves for us forgiveness, eternal life, and the promise of Heaven. A prayer of salvation is simply talking with God, telling Him that we believe that we are sinners, that Jesus Christ paid for our sins in full when He died in our place on the cross, and that we believe that Jesus is indeed our Savior by faith. If you have never settled that decision between you and God, I invite you to do so right now by praying this simple prayer, by faith, to God:

> *Dear God, thank You for loving me. I admit that I am a sinner and that my sin separates me from You and must be punished by death.*
>
> *Thank You for sending Your only Son, Jesus Christ, to die on the cross for me in order to pay for my sins in full with His death. I open the door of my heart and invite Jesus Christ to come into my life and to be my Savior. Thank You, Jesus, for coming into my life and for giving me the free gift of eternal life and the promise of living with You in Heaven forever! In Jesus' name I pray, amen.*

▪ RECEIVING THE HOLY SPIRIT

There is a great promise in Romans 10:13 that declares, "*for 'Everyone who calls on the name of the Lord will be saved.'*" Therefore, if you have cried out and called upon Jesus Christ to forgive you and save you, this promise is for you! But it gets even better!

> *"Peter replied, 'Repent and be baptized, every one of you, in the name of Jesus Christ for the forgiveness of your sins. And you will receive the gift of the Holy Spirit.'"*
> *-Acts 2:38*

The Bible makes it crystal clear that all who believe in and receive Jesus Christ as their Savior also immediately, simultaneously, and permanently receive the Holy Spirit in their lives as well! Listen to these great promises to that end:

- *"Peter replied, 'Repent and be baptized, every one of you, in the name of Jesus Christ for the forgiveness of your sins. And you will receive the gift of the Holy Spirit.'" -Acts 2:38*
- *"Because you are His sons, God sent the Spirit of His Son into our hearts, the Spirit who calls out, 'Abba Father.'" -Galatians 4:6*
- *"In him [Jesus] you also, when you heard the word of truth, the gospel of your salvation, and believed in him, were sealed with the promised Holy Spirit ... ." -Ephesians 1:13, ESV, clarification added*
- *"Anyone who does not have the Spirit of Christ does not belong to Him."-Romans 8:9b, ESV*

Again, when you received Jesus Christ by faith as your Savior, the Holy Spirit immediately, simultaneously, and permanently indwelt your life, ushering in the Person, presence, and power of God into your body and into your life forever and ever! As the Apostle Paul explains in 2 Corinthians 9:15, *"Thanks be to God for his indescribable gift!"*

▪ RELATING TO THE HOLY SPIRIT

As we learned earlier, the Holy Spirit of God is a Person with intellect, emotion, and will, who is to be pursued, known, loved, and related to on a daily basis! Since that is true, how do we go about pursuing, developing, maintaining, and deepening our personal one-on-one relationship with the Holy Spirit? Very much like any human relationship, there are things we can do to harm a relationship and things we can do to enrich a relationship with God the Holy Spirit.

Very simply, the scriptural warnings against those actions that will harm our relationship with the Holy Spirit are few and very clear:

- We are not to **sin** against the Holy Spirit by rejecting God's grace in His offer of salvation in the gospel (Matthew 12:31-32).
- We are not to **grieve** the Holy Spirit (to cause Him pain, sadness, or sorrow) by our sinful actions against God and disobedience to His Word and, in this particular context, sinning against fellow believers (Ephesians 4:30).

- We are not to **quench** the Holy Spirit by failing to rely upon Him or by denying or diminishing His activity (gifts, fruits, power) in our lives (1 Thessalonians 5:19).

The three examples above reflect ways that we have the ability to harm or diminish our daily relationship with the Holy Spirit. On a more positive note, how can we enhance and improve our daily relationship or "walk" with the Person of the Holy Spirit? How does the Holy Spirit desire to come alongside us and help us to live a supernaturally empowered life that is pleasing to God? The answer is simple: it's all about recognizing our absolute spiritual poverty, weakness, and lack of vitality apart from a totally dependent, moment-by-moment, daily, abiding relationship with the Holy Spirit.

So how do we do that?

The Bible gives us several clear instructions to help us know how to enhance the harmony and efficacy of our relationship with the Holy Spirit. Obviously, we are not to do anything on a daily basis that would grieve, quench, or sin against the Person of the Holy Spirit. And on the positive side, Scripture encourages us to do several things to demonstrate our total dependence upon the Person of the Holy Spirit for living a fruitful and successful, Christ-honoring life every single day of our lives. It is all about two things: maintaining a close relationship and total dependency upon the Holy Spirit to live an obedient and God-honoring life.

▪ FINISH BY THE SPIRIT: A DAILY FAITH JOURNEY

In Galatians 3, Paul warns the Galatian believers by asking them six questions about their relationship with the Holy Spirit in five brief verses:

> *"You foolish Galatians! Who has bewitched you? Before your very eyes Jesus Christ was clearly portrayed as crucified. I would like to learn just one thing from you: Did you receive the Spirit by the works of the law, or by believing what you heard? Are you so foolish? After beginning by means of the Spirit, are you now trying to finish by means of the flesh? Have you experienced so much in vain—if it really was in vain? So again I ask, does God give you his Spirit and work miracles among you by the works of the law, or by your believing what you heard?" -Galatians 3:1-5*

Paul begins by reminding us that the Holy Spirit is received into our lives by believing in Jesus Christ by faith and not by our works.

And then, he exhorts the Galatian Christians to rely upon the Holy Spirit to indwell them and to work miracles in and through their lives by faith and not by their own efforts, works, or strength. In other words, we are to live the Christian life in a daily faith-dependent relationship upon the Holy Spirit to *"work miracles"* in and through our lives by His supernatural power every day. We start the Christian life by faith, and we must live and finish the Christian life through daily faith in the Holy Spirit, who lives in us and supernaturally (miraculously) works through us by means of His gifts, fruit, and power!

"BE FILLED WITH THE SPIRIT"

OVERFLOWING RESOURCES AND PRESENCE

In Ephesians 5:18, the Apostle Paul exhorts the Ephesian believers with a command, *"And do not get drunk with wine, for that is dissipation, but be filled with the Spirit (NASB)."* The phrase, *"be filled with the Spirit"* is a present, plural, passive imperative, meaning that God commands (not an option!) you, me, and all believers to continuously go on being filled with the Holy Spirit! It is a must! It is essential! It is a constant! And we cannot do it ourselves! By faith, we must continuously depend upon the divine Person of the Holy Spirit to be filled to the full, fully supplied, or as it were, overflowing with the indwelling Spirit of God! This filling or overflow of the Spirit is exactly what Jesus had in mind when He proclaimed, *"'Whoever believes in me, as Scripture has said, rivers of living water will flow from within them.' By this he meant the Spirit, whom those who believed in him were*

later to receive. Up to that time the Spirit had not been given,
since Jesus had not yet been glorified (John 7:38-39)."

> "The Spirit-filled life is not a special, deluxe
> edition of Christianity. It is part and parcel
> of the total plan of God for His people."
> -A.W. Tozer

Since we are commanded to continuously go on being filled with the Holy Spirit, this clearly implies that we may choose to obey (or disobey) this command! Obviously, sinning against, grieving, or quenching the Spirit will significantly, if not completely, hinder the powerful flow of the ministry of the Holy Spirit through our lives. On the positive side, what can we do to increase or enhance the overflow of the Spirit's work through our lives? The short answer is to simply pray daily and continuously ask God to fill us to overflowing with the Person, presence, power, and ministries of the Holy Spirit!

My friend and longtime associate at East-West, Dr. Joe Wall, recently reminded me that, according to Scripture, there are two primary ways in which the Holy Spirit fills us.

First, the Holy Spirit supernaturally fills us with wisdom, understanding, and the knowledge of God's will (Colossians

1:9) and fills our lives and our speech with praise, worship, and thanksgiving to God (Ephesians 5:18-20).

These passages both contain the Greek word *pleroo*, which means that the entirety of our lives should be constantly filled and overflowing with the supernatural character of God.

Second, the Holy Spirit also fills us with supernatural power for ministry, most notably for the proclamation and advancement of the gospel as we see in Acts 2:4 (miraculously speaking in unknown languages), Acts 4:8 (Peter preaching boldly before the Sanhedrin), and Acts 4:31 (believers speaking the Word of God boldly). These verses contain the Greek word *pletho*, which carries the meaning of our being filled with supernatural power for ministry.

Both types of filling are a result of the supernatural indwelling of God the Holy Spirit, and both are the result of our trust in, obedience to, and reliance upon God to so fill and use us.

In Luke's Gospel, one of Jesus' disciples asked Him to teach them how to pray. In response, Jesus taught them what we refer to as the Lord's Prayer, followed by a parable that encourages greater boldness (shameless audacity) in prayer with an exhortation to repeatedly *"ask," "seek,"* and *"knock"* (Matthew 7:7). Jesus compares the relative goodness of human fathers to the absolute and perfect goodness of God, our Heavenly Father, when He says, *"If you then, though you are evil, know how to give good gifts to your children, how much more will your Father in heaven give the Holy Spirit to those who ask him (Luke 11:13)!"*

The clear message here is that the great gift that our Father delights to give to all of His children is the Holy Spirit *"to those who ask Him!"* Since all born-again believers already have the Holy Spirit permanently indwelling them, the prayer we should pray every day is to ask God to so fill us with His Holy Spirit that we are overflowing with His supernatural presence, power, gifts, and fruits, so that *"rivers of living water"* will flow through our lives to bless and serve those around us on a daily basis (John 7:38).

"WALK BY THE SPIRIT"

SUPERNATURAL POWER

In Galatians 5, the chapter known most famously for the *"fruit of the Spirit (Galatians 5:22-23)"* and that also contains the acts (or fruit) of the flesh (Galatians 5:19-21), there are surprisingly no commands related to putting on or putting off these good or bad fruits respectively. But there is a clear command that precedes both of these lists in Galatians 5, and that is the command to *"walk by the Spirit (Galatians 5:16)."* Our focus should not be on the fruit, whether bad or good, but on our relationship with the Holy Spirit, who alone can empower us to say no to the fleshly fruit and to abundantly bear the Spirit's fruit. You will not succeed on your own initiative or power in putting off the deeds of your flesh or in manifesting the fruit of the Spirit. No, that is the Spirit's work to be done in and through you as you focus on your obedience to the command to *"walk by the Spirit."*

> "If we walk in the Spirit daily, surrendered to His power, we have the right to expect anything we need from God. The Holy Spirit living within us and speaking to us ought to be the natural, normal lifestyle of believers."
> -Charles Stanley

What does this mean? How do we *"walk by the Spirit"?* This is another command to be obeyed—meaning that we are to walk or live daily by faith in full dependence upon the Holy Spirit to provide the supernatural power required for us to put away fleshly desires and deeds and to demonstrate the Spirit's fruit consistently through our lives. We are to walk every moment of our lives relying on the Spirit's power to lead us in paths of righteousness, for His name's sake (Psalm 23:3). After all, He is the **Holy** Spirit, and every path He will lead us to walk upon will be holy, righteous, pure, and good!

"BE LED BY THE SPIRIT"

DIVINE GUIDANCE

There are innumerable passages in the Old and New Testaments about the Holy Spirit guiding, advising, and otherwise directing God's people (Psalm 143:10; Isaiah 48:16; Ezekiel 37:1; Matthew 4:1; Mark 1:12; Luke 2:27; Acts 8:29, 10:19-20, 11:12, 13:2, etc.).

In Galatians 5:18, Paul writes, *"But if you are led by the Spirit, you are not under the law."* This does not mean that we are against the law (antinomianism) but rather that we have an internal (intrinsic) versus an external (extrinsic) Source guiding our lives, and that is the indwelling Holy Spirit. The Holy Spirit teaches us all things and reminds us of Jesus' teachings (John 14:26). We are to walk in constant dependence upon the Holy Spirit to guide us as we live our lives devoted to God. We do this by seeking God's guidance through prayer (James 1:5), reading God's Word

(Psalm 119:105), seeking counsel from spiritual leaders (Acts 15:6-7), all the while waiting upon the Holy Spirit to confirm and direct our paths (Acts 15:28, 16:6-10). This must be our daily practice, being constantly submissive to the leading of the Holy Spirit in our lives—not just in times of extraordinary and very significant life decisions but in every minute of every day as we walk in humble surrender to and dependency upon the Holy Spirit to lead and guide our lives.

▪ TRUSTING THE VOICE OF THE SPIRIT

My friend, Jason Uptmore, is a missions pastor in San Antonio. A few years ago, he gave a sermon illustrating the practice of walking by, being led by, and keeping in step with the Spirit in our daily lives.

Jason comes from a fishing family. Every summer, his family would go to the coast to fish their hearts out. Jason joked that fishing is a "holy" activity because the Scriptures describe Jesus and the disciples fishing often. So when Jason goes fishing, he says, "I'm just imitating my Savior!"

But as often as he and his family fished, Jason was never great at actually catching fish. He mainly enjoyed the activity of casting a line, and if he caught anything, it was a bonus! One year, Jason, his father, and his brother decided to hire a guide to show them how to catch fish. Their fishing guide—a large, intimidating looking fellow—took them out into the water and said, "I'm going to cast your line out for you, and I'm going to tell you when that fish is on the line—but don't set that hook until I tell you." The instruction sounded easy enough, but the three men had all developed bad fishing habits. The guide would cast out their lines, and as soon as the men felt a tug, they would rip the hook right out of the fish's mouth. They didn't wait for their guide. The guide would shake his head and say, "Quit depending on your own instincts, and wait for my command."

After some time and plenty of failed attempts, the men eventually learned to trust the guide's leadership and wait for his voice to tell them when to act. It took repetition, but soon, they were catching fish! Their bad habits were being replaced with new ones, and it resulted in a successful fishing trip.

Walking by, being led by, and keeping in step with the Spirit takes repetition and practice. Allowing the Spirit to guide us requires trusting His voice, His authority, His leadership. Doing so will lead to fruitful experiences that glorify our Father. Through repetition, we will eventually unlearn the bad practices that have produced the fruits of the flesh.

"KEEP IN STEP WITH THE SPIRIT"

FINDING HEAVEN'S PACE

Paul goes on to say, *"Since we live by the Spirit, let us keep in step with the Spirit (Galatians 5:25)."* The source of our spiritual life was and is the Holy Spirit, and so Paul argues that since this is true, we should *"keep in step with the Spirit,"* who is the source of our life. The idea here is of allowing the Holy Spirit, by our careful and constant attention, to direct our steps so that we do not fall out of line with Him— whether rushing ahead, lagging behind, or going off course to the left or to the right. The image here is of an orderly march in which we are to keep our eyes on our pacesetter, the Holy Spirit, to establish our pace and order our steps— our very lives—on a moment-by-moment and daily basis!

▪ THE SPIRIT'S PERMANENT PRESENCE

> For the believer, the question is not whether
> the Holy Spirit will **leave** you but whether you
> will allow the holy spirit to **lead** you daily.

As we look to keep in step with the Spirit, it is important to know where the Spirit will be on this journey. In the Old Testament, we see that the Holy Spirit's presence was **selective** and **temporary**. Samuel told Saul, as he anointed him king over the Israelites, that the Spirit of the Lord would come powerfully upon him and that God would be with him (1 Samuel 10:6-7).

A few chapters later, Saul disobeyed God, and the Lord rejected him as king.

> *"Now the Spirit of the Lord had **departed from Saul**, and an evil spirit from the Lord tormented him." -1 Samuel 16:14, emphasis added*

The Holy Spirit, which had once been powerfully upon Saul, had turned away from him. Even David, Saul's successor, knew that God could remove His Spirit from him.

"Do not cast me from your presence or take your Holy Spirit from me." -Psalm 51:11

So, there was a time when God's Spirit was given **selectively** and **temporarily**.

But then, the Apostle John, *"the disciple whom Jesus loved (John 13:23),"* captured an amazing teaching by Jesus about the Holy Spirit:

> *"'I will ask the Father, and He will give you another Helper, so that **He may be with you forever**; the Helper is the Spirit of truth, whom the world cannot receive, because it does not see Him or know Him; but you know Him because He remains with you and will be in you. I will not leave you as orphans; I am coming to you.'" -John 14:16-18, NASB, emphasis added*

For the first time, Jesus promises that the Helper—the Holy Spirit—will forever be with all those who put their saving faith in Christ. What was once a temporary presence is now **permanent**.

And the Spirit's presence is also **universal**. Read what Paul wrote to the church in Corinth:

*"For we were **all** baptized by one Spirit so as to form one body—whether Jews or Gentiles, slave or free—and we were **all** given the one Spirit to drink." -1 Corinthians 12:13, emphasis added*

Rather than selectively resting upon a few individuals, the Holy Spirit is given freely to **all** born-again believers.

Again, in the Old Testament, God gave the Holy Spirit **selectively and temporarily.** Then in the New Testament, by the time Jesus is walking on Earth, God gives the Holy Spirit **universally and permanently**—this is true for all born-again believers.

For the believer, the question is not whether the Holy Spirit will **leave** you but whether you will allow the Holy Spirit to **lead** you daily.

If there is any apprehension to allowing the permanently and universally given Holy Spirit to lead in your life daily, just remember the words recorded in John 14:16-18.

In these three brief verses, Jesus makes many astounding promises to His disciples, which are equally applicable to you and me and to all who have received Jesus Christ by faith as their Savior!

- God will give you the Holy Spirit (John 14:16).

- The Holy Spirit will be your Helper (John 14:16).
- The Holy Spirit will be with you *forever* (John 14:16).
- The Holy Spirit is the Spirit of truth (John 14:17).
- The world (unbelievers) cannot receive the Holy Spirit (John 14:17).
- You can, and will, know the Holy Spirit (John 14:17).
- The Holy Spirit *remains with* you forever (John 14:17).
- The Holy Spirit *remains inside* you forever (John 14:17).
- The Holy Spirit adopts you and indwells you (John 14:17) daily as the Spirit of Jesus (John 14:18).

What an array of magnificent promises are granted to each of us by Jesus Himself in this passage! Most significantly is the synonym Jesus gives to the Holy Spirit when He refers to Him as *"another Helper"* using the Greek word *parakleton*, which is often translated as Helper, Comforter, Advocate, Counselor, or Intercessor. Literally, it means someone "called to be close beside you to help you."

Thayer's Greek Lexicon describes the role of the Holy Spirit as the One "destined to take the place of Christ with the apostles [and with you] (after His ascension to the Father), to lead them to a deeper knowledge of gospel truth, and to give them the divine strength needed to enable them to undergo

trials and persecutions on behalf of the divine Kingdom …
(Thayer's Greek Lexicon: Strong's New Testament, page
3875)." You are not alone! You will never be alone! Having
received the free gift of eternal life through faith in Jesus,
you immediately and eternally enjoy the presence of God's
Holy Spirit residing in you as your Helper, Comforter,
Counselor, Intercessor, and Advocate!

▪ THE SPIRIT'S GOAL: YOUR TOTAL TRANSFORMATION

In his excellent book, "Flying Closer to the Flame," Chuck
Swindoll reflects upon the radical transformation that took
place when Jesus' original disciples were transformed from
a group of "troubled, confused, bothered, disloyal, fearful,
doubting" men to those who later "turned the world upside
down (pages 39, 41)." Swindoll goes on to describe what he
calls a four-fold transformation that I hope would describe
our lives as well:

- "First, their human frailties were transformed into
  supernatural gifts and abilities."
- "Second, their fearful reluctance was transformed
  into bold confidence."
- "Third, their fears and intimidation were transformed into a sense of invincibility."

- "Fourth, their lonely, grim feelings of abandonment were transformed into joyful perseverance (pages 43-48)."

> "The Holy Spirit's main ministry is not to give thrills but to create in us Christlike character."
> -J.I. Packer

This utter and complete transformation is exactly what the indwelling Person of the Holy Spirit intends for your life as well. God has graciously given you the Holy Spirit as His permanent indwelling presence to transform your life: to help you, to strengthen you, to guide you, to counsel you, to comfort you, and to pray for you! The Person of the Holy Spirit is your constant Companion, your new and forever Best Friend, your complete supply of everything you need to live a fruitful, joyful, successful, surrendered, holy, God-pleasing, and God-honoring life! But we must maintain and enjoy a moment-by-moment awareness of and engagement with Him as a divine Person in an abiding, daily relationship. As in any healthy interpersonal and successful relationship, we accomplish the maximum mutual benefit of this relationship by constantly obeying God's Word and:

- Not sinning against the Spirit;
- Not grieving the Spirit;

- Not quenching the Spirit's gifts and fruit in our lives;
- Living in daily faith dependence upon the Spirit;
- Surrendering to the Spirit's overflowing presence;
- Seeking the Spirit's guidance;
- Relying on the Spirit's power;
- Observing and maintaining the Spirit's pace;
- Enjoying the Spirit's constant presence;
- And embracing the Spirit's total transformation.

It's all about desiring and maintaining a surrendered and submitted daily relationship with God, the Holy Spirit, who indwells you with the presence of Jesus and the presence of the Father to bless you and to help you to live your best possible life ever! Thanks be to God!

MY PERSONAL PRACTICE

I realize that I've written much about how you can experience the Holy Spirit personally in your own life every day. Let me close this section with a very simple exhortation and application. The exhortation is this: if you have not already done so, I urge you to receive Jesus Christ as your Savior; and in so doing, receive the Holy Spirit, both as free gifts to you of God's unfathomable love and grace (see pages 30-32).

The application is simply sharing how I begin every day of my life with a desire and an intention to live a life of total surrender and abandonment to the Holy Spirit.

In 1 Corinthians 6:19-20, Paul reminds us, *"Do you not know that your bodies are temples of the Holy Spirit, who is in you, whom you have received from God? You are not your own; you were bought at a price. Therefore honor God with your bodies."*

In response to these truths and to this command, I begin each day by getting down on my knees before the Lord, confessing my sins, thanking Him for forgiving and cleansing me, and for indwelling me with the Person of the Holy Spirit. Then, I resurrender my entire life to God, and I ask the Holy Spirit to fill me with His Holy Person, with His abiding presence, with His resurrection power, with the manifestation of the spiritual gifts He has given me, and to demonstrate the fruit of the Spirit in and through my life today. I ask the Holy Spirit to fill me, to empower me, to guide me, and to essentially live His holy life in and through my mortal body throughout the day ahead. Sometimes, I'll prayerfully sing the lyrics of a hymn like "Take My Life and Let It Be" by Frances Ridley Havergal. Or I'll sing aloud the simple prayer, "Spirit of the Living God, fall afresh on me / Spirit of the Living God, fall afresh on me / Melt me, mold me, fill me, use me / Spirit of the Living God, fall afresh on me." At other times, I'll simply recite the words of Psalm 139:23-24, *"Search me, God, and know my heart; test me and know my anxious thoughts. See if there is any offensive way in me, and lead me in the way everlasting."*

After that, I typically pray for my wife, our children, our grandchildren, friends, neighbors, East-West staff members, and ministry and other personal needs. As the day progresses, the Holy Spirit inevitably convicts me of sin (as I am reminded that, *"as a living sacrifice (Romans 12:1),"* I crawled off the altar again!), which I immediately confess, repent of, and resurrender and submit my life to God, the Holy Spirit. It's all about a daily, moment-by-moment, close, and abiding relationship with the Person of the Holy Spirit of God. This abiding relationship is freely offered to you, as well, through the generous love and immeasurable grace of God!

IN CONCLUSION

It is not difficult to live the Christian life apart from the Person, presence, power, and purpose of the Holy Spirit—it is completely impossible! We must be utterly dependent upon the Person, presence, power, and purpose of the Holy Spirit in order to live supernatural lives that bring glory to God. The Prophet Zechariah reminds us of this.

> *"'This is the word of the Lord to Zerubbabel:*
> *"Not by might nor by power, but by my Spirit,"*
> *says the Lord Almighty.'" -Zechariah 4:6*

What East-West is seeing God do as disciples of Jesus are multiplied in spiritually dark places—whether in Dallas, Texas, or to the ends of the Earth—is simply by the power of the gospel, the power of the Word of God, and the power of the Holy Spirit. It is a privilege for each of us to take part in God's incredible mission!

In closing, I want to leave you with five applications in regard to the Holy Spirit in your life.

First, because the **priority** of the Holy Spirit is to bring glory to God the Father and to Jesus Christ, be careful not to seek glory for yourself as God uses you with His supernatural presence to produce fruit. Be careful not to glorify the Holy Spirit apart from the Father and the Son!

Second, because the Holy Spirit is a **Person**, pursue an intimate daily relationship with Him. Get to know Him better—just as you do the Father and the Son, Jesus Christ.

Third, because the Holy Spirit is always **present** in your life, be careful to live a life of holiness. Do not grieve the Holy Spirit by giving into the ever-present temptations and flesh patterns that we all face.

Fourth, because the Holy Spirit is the one and only source of **power** in your life, submit and surrender to Him daily as your only source of supernatural spiritual power. This enables you to please Him.

Fifth and last, because the Holy Spirit's **purpose** in your life is to equip and empower you for bold and effective witness to the gospel, ask the Holy Spirit to guide you to engage with both local and international ministry opportunities to equip and engage you to share the gospel both locally and globally.

As I close, this is my prayer for you.

Thank You, Jesus, for sending the Person of Your Holy Spirit to indwell us with Your presence forever, giving us the power to live a truly fruitful and supernatural life.

"For this reason I kneel before the Father, from whom every family in Heaven and on Earth derives its name. I pray that out of his glorious riches he may strengthen you with power through his Spirit in your inner being, so that Christ may dwell in your hearts through faith. And I pray that you, being rooted and established in love, may have power, together with all the Lord's holy people, to grasp how wide and long and high and deep is the love of Christ, and to know this love that surpasses knowledge—that you may be filled to the measure of all the fullness of God.

"Now to him who is able to do immeasurably more than all we ask or imagine, according to his power that is at work within us, to him be glory in the church and in Christ Jesus throughout all generations, for ever and ever! Amen." -Ephesians 3:14-21

May you go forth filled with the Holy Spirit to fruitfully glorify God through your Spirit-empowered life. To God be all the glory. Amen.

ABBREVIATED BIBLIOGRAPHY

1   Berding, Kenneth. *Walking in the Spirit*. Wheaton, IL: Crossway, 2011.

2   Bridges, Jerry. *The Fruitful Life*. Colorado Springs, CO: NavPress, 2018.

3   Bright, Bill. *10 Basic Steps Toward Christian Maturity: Step 1: The Christian Adventure*. Orlando, FL: New Life Resources, 2007.

4   Bright, Bill. *How You Can Be Filled With the Holy Spirit*. Orlando, FL: New Life Publications, 2002.

5   Bright, Bill. *The Holy Spirit, the Key to Supernatural Living*. San Bernardino, CA: Here's Life Publishers, 1980.

6   Chan, Francis. *Forgotten God: Reversing Our Tragic Neglect of the Holy Spirit*. Colorado Springs, CO: David C Cook, 2009.

7   Denison, Jim. *Empowered: A Guide to Experiencing the Power of the Holy Spirit.* Dallas, TX: Denison Forum.

8   Evans, Tony. *Free at Last: Experiencing True Freedom Through Your Identity in Christ.* Chicago: Moody Press, 2001.

9   Harper, A. F. *Holiness and High Country.* Kansas City, MO: Beacon Hill Press, 2003.

10 Howard, David M. *By the Power of the Holy Spirit.* Downers Grove, IL: InterVarsity Press, 1973.

11 Jeremiah, David. *God in You: Releasing the Power of the Holy Spirit in Your Life.* Sisters, OR: Multnomah Publishers, 1998.

12 Kenneson, Philip D. *Life on the Vine: Cultivating the Fruit of the Spirit.* Downers Grove, IL: IVP Books, 2009.

13 Mainprize, Don. *How to Enjoy the Christian Life.* Grand Rapids, MI: Zondervan Publishing Co., 1966.

14 Oswalt, John N. *Called To Be Holy.* Anderson, IN: Warner Press, 1999.

15 Riggs, Charlie. *Learning to Walk With God.* Minneapolis, MN: World Wide Publications, 1988.

16 Simpson, A. B. *Walking in the Spirit: A Series of Arresting Addresses on the Subject of the Holy Spirit in Christian Experience.* Harrisburg, PA: Christian Publications, 1952.

17 Smith, Steve. *Spirit Walk—Special Edition: The Extraordinary Power of Acts for Ordinary People.* Littleton, CO: William Carey Publishing, 2020.

18 Stott, John R.W. *Baptism and Fullness: The Work of the Holy Spirit Today.* Downers Grove, IL: InterVarsity Press, 2006.

19 Swindoll, Charles R. *Embraced by the Spirit: The Untold Blessings of Intimacy with God.* Grand Rapids, MI: Zondervan, 2010.

20 Tozer, A.W. *Tozer: Mystery of the Holy Spirit.* Newberry, FL: Bridge-Logos, 2007.

21 *Understanding the Holy Spirit Made Easy.* Peabody, MA: Hendrickson Publishers, 2018.

22 Wemp, C. Sumner. *How on Earth can I be Spiritual?* Nashville, TN: Thomas Nelson, 1990.

23 White, John. *When the Spirit Comes with Power: Signs and Wonders Among God's People.* Downers Grove, IL: InterVarsity Press, 2009.

24 Wright, Christopher J. H. *Cultivating the Fruit of the Spirit: Growing in Christlikeness.* Downers Grove, IL: IVP Books, 2017.

ABOUT KURT NELSON

As President and Chief Executive Officer of East-West, Kurt Nelson provides leadership and oversight to all worldwide ministry endeavors in the 40-plus countries in which East-West currently operates. After serving with East-West for 13 years, Kurt became President and CEO in June 2010 and has served with East-West for more than 26 years.

Kurt serves on the Board of Directors for East-West, the Dallas Christian Leadership Prayer Breakfast, EFCA, and The Moody Center.

Kurt received his undergraduate degree from the University of North Carolina, his Master of Theology in World

Missions from Dallas Theological Seminary, and his Doctor of Ministry in Missions Leadership from Columbia International University.

Kurt and his wife, Pat, have been married for more than 35 years and have nine children (three of whom were adopted from Russia, and one who went to Heaven in 2021), six grandsons (one who went to Heaven in 2020) and one granddaughter.

ABOUT EAST-WEST

East-West has one consuming passion—to make God known among every nation, every tribe, every language, and every people. More than 3 billion people worldwide have yet to hear the gospel, and it's our mission to go to the ends of the Earth to reach them. Our aim is to shine God's light to overcome spiritual darkness.

To maximize our impact for the Kingdom of Heaven, East-West focuses on four foundational strategies within its mission:

MOBILIZE THE BODY OF CHRIST: We send the Church to the spiritually darkest places in the world.

EVANGELIZE THE LOST: We bring the gospel to unreached people groups and limited access areas.

EQUIP LOCAL BELIEVERS: We train nationals to reach the lost in their own communities.

MULTIPLY DISCIPLES AND CHURCHES: We raise up disciples and churches to multiply more disciples and churches.

VISION: The vision of East-West is to glorify God by multiplying followers of Jesus in the spiritually darkest areas of the world.

MISSION: The mission of East-West is to mobilize the Body of Christ to evangelize the lost and equip local believers to multiply disciples and churches among the unreached.

CORE VALUES

PASSION FOR JESUS: The pursuit of Jesus—as our Savior, as our sovereign King, and as our example—is the motivation behind our lives and our ministry efforts.

PASSION FOR GRACE: The gospel of grace is our greatest joy and is the message we relentlessly declare through our actions and words.

PASSION FOR THE SPIRITUALLY DARKEST PLACES: The redemptive power of the gospel compels us to take the name of Jesus where it is unknown, unmentionable, and unwanted.

PASSION FOR BOLD ACTION: God's demonstration of bold action to rescue the lost necessitates our own creative, incessant, and boldly courageous initiative to fulfill His Great Commission—no matter the cost.

HISTORY

East-West began because two men couldn't resist the call of Christ's great mission: go into the world and make disciples. East-West's founders John Maisel and Bud Toole spent the 1980s secretly traveling behind the Iron Curtain to train students in biblical education.

Then, Communist governments began to collapse, resulting in the fall of the Iron Curtain in 1989. The 300 million people who had been taught the doctrines of atheism began to seek real answers out of their spiritual hunger. A new need arose—to train church planters and pastors in nations characterized by restricted Christian activity. John and Bud responded to the call.

In May 1993, East-West was established to train and mentor faithful and reliable national pastors to become catalysts for indigenous church growth—reaching the lost with the gospel, equipping new believers, and multiplying reproducible churches.

Since 1993, the Lord has been faithful in expanding the reach of East-West. From two men standing at its founding, East-West has grown to hundreds of staff members and thousands of national partners. Today, East-West works in limited access nations and among unreached people groups in more than 40 countries across 10 major world regions. From the remote mountains of South Asia to the suburbs in North America, we work wherever the unreached are.

In pursuing our vision and mission, we recognize that we are only a part of the bigger story that God Himself is writing.

"After this I looked, and there before me was a great multitude that no one could count, from every nation, tribe, people and language, standing before the throne and before the Lamb."-Revelation 7:9a

GET INVOLVED

It's time to discover your role in the Great Commission. Consider the following ways you can partner with East-West in God's Kingdom work.

 **PRAY:** Prayer moves the mission. God works when we pray, which is why East-West is committed to passionate, consistent prayer for the unreached and our missionaries and national partners who serve among them. Prayer is our most powerful weapon against the kingdom of darkness; therefore, it is the greatest gift you can give to our ministry. You can join us in the important work of praying for those living in the throes of spiritual darkness as we seek to reach them with the good news of Jesus in a way that transforms their lives forever. Learn more about how you can partner with us in prayer at **www.eastwest. org/pray.**

GIVE: Your gift to East-West has eternal value. It continually expands our reach and multiples our impact as we seek to take the gospel to the lost. Each gift is an investment to reach the darkest areas of the world with the light of God's Word. With East-West, you are not investing in a fleeting kingdom of man but in an eternal Kingdom that cannot be shaken. You can give to the general ministry of East-West, to a missionary, to a region, or to a short-term mission team member. You can give now at **www.eastwest.org/give.**

GO: Join the movement of the gospel throughout the nations by partnering with East-West on the field. Because the Great Commission is for every believer, we're committed to empowering the global Church to reach the unreached. Through short-term teams, missionary deployments, and mid-term opportunities, we train and send people just like you to take the gospel where it's never been. As believers go, we are witnessing God's Kingdom invade the spiritually darkest areas of the world. Explore the different ways you can go with East-West at **www.eastwest.org/go.**

Made in the USA
Monee, IL
29 April 2023